School children in London marching to a local railway station on the second day of the great evacuation.

THE COVER: *Apprehensive evacuees waiting to be led onto buses.*

PHOTOGRAPHS: *The wartime photographs featured in this book are the property of the London-based Popperfote Image Library. The company is the U.K.'s oldest and largest independently owned image library. Established in 1934, the company has in excess of 14 million images covering 150 years of photographic history. The North American representative for Popperfoto is Philadelphia-based Robertstock.com.*

Note for Librarians: A cataloguing record for this book is available from Library and Archives Canada at www.collectionscanada.ca/amicus/index-e.html. ISBN-978-1-4251-2052-8

BOOK SALES:

Books can be purchased from the author as follows: **Single copy sales:** *Send cheque for $16.00 to Brian Perks, 99 Switzer Drive, Oshawa, Ontario, L1G 3J5. Cost covers shipping to a Canadian address (bubble-wrap envelope, postage, handling) and additionally includes GST.* **Multiple-copy sales:** *Send e-mail to ebperks@yahoo.ca. Indicate number of copies required and preferred payment method – i.e. via purchase order or direct payment by cheque. Volume price will be e-mailed to sender. Include mail address and telephone number when ordering.*

WEBSITE: www.brian-perks.com

Books can be additionally ordered via Trafford Publishing. Visit: trafford.com/07-0456

Introduction

At the outbreak of the Second World War, the British Government urged women and children to move away from large areas of population. As a consequence, thousands left the major cities. They moved to the towns and villages of rural England.

It was a voluntary exodus. Parents had the option of staying in the cities with their children but few chose to do so. The government swayed people by predicting that German aircraft would kill thousands of people in the early days of the war. A figure of 4,000,000 civilian casualties was predicted for the city of London alone.

While the majority of women and children went to live with relatives and friends there were those in the cities who did not have the means to effect their own evacuation. The government stepped in. It organized a mass evacuation of women, children, and infirm citizens such as the blind and disabled.

It was the biggest mass evacuation of civilians that had ever been undertaken in the history of the United Kingdom. In a four day period, September 1 to 4, 1939, more than 1,385,000 people were evacuated by the government.

The evacuation, code-named "Operation Pied Piper", was more accurately two evacuations. The first was for school aged children who were mostly five to fourteen years old. **Parents were excluded**. The children were given the designation "unaccompanied"– meaning that a parent, relative, or an adult friend of the family could not participate.

The second evacuation was for mothers, children who had not yet reached the age of five, expectant mothers, and the infirm. The under-five children stayed with their mothers.

The five to fourteen year olds were by far the biggest group. They numbered 827,000 and were evacuated in the following manner:

Each child was identified with a luggage label that was attached to a part of their clothing. They were given a gas mask and a small amount of food and were allowed a limited supply of clothing. With the exception of the gas mask that was carried in a small cardboard box, the "luggage" of each child was confined to one small suitcase, or a pillowcase,

At the railway station: *A girl with a brown paper carrier bag takes a quick look back.*

or simply a brown paper carrier bag with a string handle.

Parents took their children to "departure points", frequently a school playground, and left them there. Buses and trains were then used to move the children to various destinations in the country. Upon arrival they were assembled, like cattle, on a village green or inside a community hall to be "viewed and selected."

Rural inhabitants looked the children over, picked one (or two) and took them home – to look after them for the duration of the war. **There was no central master plan for child care.** Lodging was not pre-assigned. Guardians were not pre-selected. It was a human lottery. The good fortune or bad luck experienced by individual evacuees was a matter of chance.

Mothers, along with their off-spring and the blind and the disabled, fared better. Most local authorities had lodging pre-arranged.

Those who were most in need of government assistance lived in London. They were, collectively, the city's "working class poor." Their number made the evacuation a massive undertaking. The challenge however was successfully met. In the four day period previously mentioned, the following were evacuated from London:

Unaccompanied children --393,700; mothers and children under five – 257,000; expectant mothers – 5,600; blind and infirm persons – 2,440.

Among the unaccompanied evacuees was a 5-year-old boy who would have the misfortune to be "one of the unlucky ones." And not merely unlucky for a week, a month, or even a year. Misfortune would stay with the boy for the duration of the war – and beyond.

He would see things and experience things that would have the effect of making him a representative evacuee; his story, in a sense, reflecting not merely the pain and suffering of one child, but the trauma and pain experienced by many. "One Boy's Story" tells of that child. It's the way that I remember it.

I was the 5-year-old child.

Brian Perks

The Plight Of Wartime Child Evacuees

One Boy's Story

The British Government was partially ready for war in 1939.

Coffins were stockpiled, barrage balloons had been manufactured, gas masks had been produced, and the government had a plan in place for evacuating as many as 4,000,000 people (mostly children) into the English countryside

I was five years old. My sister Beryl was two.

I remember the way my mother sold me on the idea of being "evacuated". She was sitting on a chair and had me standing in front of her. I remember I was listening carefully but was observing, with a degree of fascination, my reflection in a large brass bucket that was used for storing coal. She said that some very bad people were going to drop something called "bombs" on houses and that a lot of people were going to be killed.

She said I was lucky because a big holiday for children had been arranged. The holiday was going to take place in the "country", a wonderful place that had lambs and ducks and chickens and haystacks and a host of other great things. It was going to be fun.

"You would like that, wouldn't you?" she asked.

I carefully thought about it, still looking at my reflection in the coal bucket. The part I didn't like was going on my own. Dad wouldn't be coming. Mum wouldn't be coming. And my sister Beryl wouldn't be coming either. My mother sensed my reluctance and talked with increased energy and enthusiasm.

I was only five but I knew enough to realize the game that was being played. She was cajoling and urging because she wanted me to accept and believe what she was telling me. There was even a hint of begging in her voice.

My heart went out to her and I gave her what she wanted. I looked away from the coal bucket, put on a brave face, and agreed that "going to the country" would be fun.

The next thing I recall, ahead of the actual

evacuation, was having to try on a gas mask.

It was an ugly looking thing that came in a small cardboard box. The box was approximately nine inches square and had string attached. You put the string over your shoulder to have the box rest at your side. This allowed your hands to be free. Like I said, the gas mask was ugly. It was made of rubber, had a pig-like snout, and was placed over the entire front area of the face. Wide straps placed behind and over the head kept it in place. There was a face plate made of a see-through material at the front of the mask.

I would have been the first to die if circumstance had ever forced me to use it. Having this monstrosity hugging against the side of my face was bad enough. But I couldn't breathe! The air didn't come through the snout the way it was supposed to. I told them it wasn't working but no one believed me.

After ripping the thing away from my face several times and protesting loudly, they finally gave up arguing with me and put the monstrosity back in its box.

The Evacuation

The day of the evacuation was by far the most terrifying experience of my young life. I don't recall

An air-raid warden *checks with a small boy to ensure that his gas mask is fitting correctly.*

how the day started but I know the moment, the exact moment, when the terror began.

There was a large outdoor area filled with noisy and boisterous children. The gas mask was slung over my shoulder and I was holding a brown paper carrier bag. I was looking around in bewilderment. *My mother had left me!* I was on my own.

How had it happened?

The noise and confusion scared me. The children around me seemed older and I didn't know any of them.

No one was taking any notice of me. It seemed that everyone around me knew someone or had a playmate. I was the solitary exception – or so it seemed.

A gigantic wave of desolation enveloped me.

I was standing there, feeling utterly wretched, staring at nothing in particular, when I suddenly saw the buses.

I could hardly believe what I was seeing.

A column of large, red, double-decker buses was inching its way toward us. The thing that had me transfixed was the lead bus. *It had two, big, wide-open eyes at the upper level.* The eyes gave the bus a monstrous appearance.

When I was older I figured out that the eyes

*This double-decker bus fell into a bomb crater
during the war. The mishap produced photographic
proof that "a bus with eyes" really did exist.*

had to be some sort of an advertisement.

I have no recollection of getting on one of the buses but that is what obviously happened. My next memory is being on a platform at a railway station. Some of the children seemed to be having a good

Evacuees show their concern and apprehension as they stare at the camera.

time but I noticed a lot of children who now had worry and fear on their faces. Some were crying.

When I finally found myself seated in the corner of a railway carriage I couldn't contain myself any longer. I, too, began to cry.

A train packed with evacuees makes a temporary stop, allowing volunteers to hand out drink.

There was a boy with ginger hair who took pity on me. He was, perhaps, seven or eight years old. He said some upbeat things and then suggested that we look inside our brown paper carrier bags. It seemed that most children had one of the bags.

There was an apple, an orange, a chocolate bar and some items of clothing inside the bag. Ginger said we should eat our chocolate bars and that seemed a good idea. He took the paper off the chocolate bar for me and I munched away, feeling a measure of relief.

I don't remember the train arriving or actually getting off the train. I seem to recall, however, sitting down on some grass after the train arrived.

My next memory is getting up and marching along with a large crowd of children. We arrived at a "green", a large open area in the middle of a village.

The road around the green was lined with people. We were herded onto the green like cattle.

All of a sudden it was very quiet. We looked at the adults and they stared back.

Then someone blew a whistle.

At first I couldn't tell what was happening because there were children all around me. But the crowd of children slowly began to thin out. I now saw that the adults were walking around the outer

Off the train: *Evacuees rest before continuing their journey.*

edge of the green, staring at the children. Once in a while one of them would stop, point at a child, and say: **"I'll take that one."** Sometimes they already had a child in tow and they would pause, point their finger, and say: "I'll take that one as well."

Ginger and I were still together and I hoped and prayed that someone would come along and take the two of us.

It was not to be.

Eventually Ginger was gone and I found myself standing, almost alone, in the middle of the green. I looked to the left and right of me and saw three or four other children some distance away. They too were looking around in bewilderment, no doubt as terrified as I had become.

I couldn't understand why I hadn't been picked.

The handle of the brown paper carrier bag was cutting into my hand but I was too afraid to let go. I stood there, immobilized by the fear and concern that was sweeping over me.

What was I going to do? Why didn't anybody want me? What was going to happen to me?

The road around the green was almost empty. On the green there had been so many children – but now they were gone. In my memory the sun was beginning to set. Whether that was really the case or not I can't say for sure. Perhaps I imagine that bit. Even more surprising is the fact that I can't remember how the experience came to an end. I have no recollection of being "selected".

The White Gate

My next memory is that of a thatched-roof cottage with climbing roses at the door. There was a flagstone path that led up to the door and there was a swinging white gate immediately ahead of the flagstone path. In this piece of memory I can see myself up on the gate, wiggling my body to make the gate swing to and fro. I don't recall falling off the gate but that's what happened.

I broke my arm.

I have a faint recollection of being in the hospital. The big thing was, however, my mother arrived! I was ecstatic. Now I'd be going home again. I'd be with my sister!

This too wasn't to be. **My mother disappeared!**

It was astonishing the way it happened. One moment she was there and the next moment she was gone. It was puzzling – and deeply upsetting. I wondered anew whether I had changed in some manner, whether there was something about me that caused people to dislike and avoid me.

The Spiders

My next memory is being in a different house with several other children. Each morning we sat around a large table and an elderly adult read a passage from the bible. We then took turns going to the outdoor toilet.

The other children, who were older, discovered that I was afraid of spiders and devised an activity that was, for them, a source of amusement. I'd be sitting on the toilet and would suddenly see a big spider crawl under the door from the outside. There would be someone outside with a stick, poking around to make one or more spiders crawl under the door. The bible-reading adult also seemed to think it was amusing – which no doubt explained why someone other than myself was allowed to be outside the house while I was using the toilet. Ordinarily, we had to go out to the toilet one at a time.

One day I devised a plan to escape the ordeal of facing the spiders. I knew there was an indoor toilet that we weren't ordinarily allowed to use. I waited until one of the older boys had gone outside and then I suddenly jumped up from the table.

"I have to go! I have to go!" I yelled.

I was told that I'd have to wait but I yelled: "I can't! I can't! I have to go!"

Though I say so myself it was a very good performance. I was told to go upstairs and use the indoor toilet. I ran up the stairs, found the bathroom, and opened the door. I then stood transfixed, unable to believe my eyes. *It was, without doubt, the most beautiful toilet and bathroom that I had ever seen.*

The walls were bright and clean, there was a rug on the floor, and everything seemed to be new and shiny. There was even a picture on the wall and two soft-looking towels were hanging from a gold bar. There was a vase with artificial flowers in it and various knick-knacks on a glass shelf.

I stood there in awe, gazing in disbelief.

A New Terror

It's perhaps far-fetched to think that my behaviour was the cause of my being moved to yet another home. Whatever the reason I next recall being in a damp, dark, slum-type row house in the town of Exmouth, in the southwest part of England. I remember, in an overall sort of way, that it was a miserable existence. I was frequently teased and bullied by boys who were older than myself.

When I was almost eight I had my first encounter with the physical reality of war. I saw, first hand, what bombs could do.

I remember that I set out for school one

morning without knowing there had been an air-raid the night before. I took my usual route and then turned at a particular corner as was my habit. The sight that met my eyes caused me to stop dead in my tracks.

The day before it had been like any other street, a narrow road with row houses on either side. Now it was a wasteland, a wide open area. There wasn't a single house left intact. The skeletal remains of perhaps five houses reared up against the sky but everything else was rubble – mounds of brick and splintered wood.

The overall effect was that the entire street had been obliterated, along with parts of an adjacent street. You could see the sky. All of it.

There was a solitary fire engine off in the distance. In the foreground were fire hoses, snaking their way up the road towards the fire engine. It was eerie. Small columns of black smoke were drifting upwards from different parts of the rubble.

I began to walk down the middle of the road, carefully avoiding the scattered bricks and hoses. My progress was then impeded by an air-raid warden who seemed to materialize out of nowhere. He told me to turn around and go to school down a different street. His face was black with smoke and his eyes were red from a lack of sleep. If he hadn't looked so exhausted I would probably have been afraid of him.

The bombing produced a new terror. There were several bomb sites in one area of town and the rubble became the stalking ground for gangs of

A single air raid *by enemy aircraft produced this swath of destruction.*

boys who ranged in age from ten to fifteen. They carried "spears" (lengths of thin wood) and threw pebbles at one another. The older boys with whom I associated formed a gang and made me their "mascot."

An air-raid warden at a bomb site offers tea to rescue workers.

There was another gang who also had a mascot. One day there was a major confrontation between the two gangs and I found myself face to face with their mascot. He was a small kid, younger than myself, with fear and terror written all over his

The flattened remains of eight row houses. Eleven *people were killed.*

face. I stared at him, awed that someone else could be even more afraid than I was. We just stared at one another. Then I turned my back and walked away. It's a funny thing – I can still see his face, years later.

The encounters became more brazen and dangerous as the days progressed. Some gang members took to carrying bicycle chains. Stones and pieces of brick replaced the pebbles.

There was one occasion when a member of our gang was captured by a rival gang. He was "tortured" with a lit cigarette. His burns weren't all that serious but it was considered a "big thing." It was now my turn to be afraid. My imagination conjured up all sorts of images as to what would happen to me if I, a mascot, was captured.

Unlovable

I believe it was some time in 1942 that my father suddenly appeared. I can't say for sure because all I remember is our walking down a road together. I seem to remember that he was holding my hand for some reason.

He suddenly said: "Brian, mummy doesn't want us any more."

He obviously must have said more than that but those are the words I remember. If I had any self-esteem at all, it died that day. At the same time a new and powerful bond was formed with my father. He, too, had somehow become unlovable. We had something in common.

In Exmouth I never had a room of my own. I slept on a narrow bed in a hallway. There was a single light bulb hanging on a wire above the bed. One night in 1942 (or perhaps it was 1943) I woke from a deep sleep as a result of someone turning on the light. It was my father! He was standing there, wearing his army uniform. I don't recall that he said anything. He picked me up and wrapped me in a blanket. And that's all I remember of the incident. I imagine that I fell back to sleep, resting against his shoulder.

My days in Exmouth were over. A new era, that of "Aunt Nell", was about to be ushered in.

Aunt Nell

A charitable person would say that my father's sister was highly strung. She was, in fact, emotionally unstable. (I did, of course, work that out much later in life).

Aunt Nell was a snob in the truest and most complete sense of the word. She had "married well" and considered herself much elevated as a result. Her world consisted of "us" and "them" – "us" being the upper middle-class and "them" every-body else who were, of course, beneath her.

When I arrived on her doorstep with my father she must have been deeply shocked. I was a dirty, grubby, unkempt kid who wiped his nose on his sleeve. I murdered the King's English whenever I opened my mouth. And I wore my socks around my ankles, close to my scuffed and worn out shoes.

My first memory of Aunt Nell is seeing her sitting at the head of the table, regal fashion, looking at me intently as the evening meal was served. There were three of us at the table; Aunt Nell, her son Michael (who was close to my own age) and myself. There was a heavy silence in the room and realizing that I was the cause of it, I decided, somewhat uncharacteristically, to try and improve the situation. There was a picture on the wall behind Aunt Nell and I said with my cockney accent: "That's a nice 'pitcher' you got on the wall there Aunt Nell."

She looked at me without any change in her expression. She then said: "Brian, a 'pitcher' is a glass jug for holding water. A **picture** is what you see hanging on the wall." She paused for a moment and then continued: "Tell me Brian, what is it you see on the wall?" I collected my wits and replied: "A **picture** Aunt Nell. A **picture.**" She gave a small nod of approval but did not relax her expression.

That was Aunt Nell.

Despite her put-on lady-like composure however she would, on occasion, fly into a rage about something. I endured several beatings and ran away twice. On both occasions the police caught up with me and I was returned to Aunt Nell.

There was one beating that I remember in particular.

Aunt Nell and Michael had this "procedure". If something went wrong and if Michael and I both denied being the culprit, Aunt Nell would give Michael a couple of slaps and tell him to tell the truth. He would vehemently state that he was telling the truth and Aunt Nell would turn her attention to me.

She would beat me in an absolute frenzy and to stop the beating I would yell out: "I did it! I did it!"

On this particular occasion the bathroom sink had been cracked in three places and was in obvious need of replacement. The "procedure" unfolded as usual but when the beating was over there was an unexpected twist:

Aunt Nell wanted to know *how* I had cracked the sink!

Now I was really scared. I wondered how

anyone could possibly crack a sink that badly. My mind raced and I came up with an answer. A favorite with children in those days were large, over-sized glass marbles. I said I had dropped some marbles in the sink and Aunt Nell accepted the explanation.

I was black and blue but immensely pleased with myself.

The Egg

There were three war-related "happenings" during the Aunt Nell era that are worthy of being recalled. The first was innocent enough. It involved an egg.

The only way to get eggs during the war (unless you lived on a farm) was to go to the store with a ration card. On this particular day Aunt Nell had sent me to the store to buy eggs. On the way home I dropped one of the eggs onto the sidewalk. The shell broke open, spilling the white of the egg and the unbroken yolk onto the sidewalk. I stood there, staring at it.

A man came along and asked me what I intended to do. I shrugged my shoulders.

"You can't leave it there son," he said. "You sure you don't want it?"

I shrugged again.

He then took a piece of card from inside his coat and scooped it off the sidewalk.

"You sure you don't want it?" he repeated.

I was too baffled to answer.

He then opened his mouth and swallowed the raw egg – all of it, the yolk, white, and bits of broken egg shell that had lodged into the white of the egg.

When I got back to Aunt Nell's I told her what had happened. I had imagined that she would be mad at me; that I would get a tongue lashing for dropping the precious egg. Instead she looked surprised (I would even say shocked) and then became very pensive. She didn't say anything. I was dismissed with a wave of her hand.

The Bomber Pilot

The second happening was full of pathos. It occurred in this manner:

A plant of the Austin Motor Company was located down the road from where Aunt Nell lived. This particular plant was building Lancaster bombers. One day I was in the vicinity of the plant and saw a strange sight.

An airman was standing on a wooden box immediately outside the main gate. Workers coming off shift were gathering around him and he was waving his arms in the air in an excited manner.

I joined the crowd, which was growing in size by the minute, to see what it was all about.

The airman looked like he had just stepped out of a Lancaster bomber after returning from a raid. He was wearing his battle dress and had on his head the tight-fitting head cap of a bomber pilot. His face had a look of personal tragedy etched into it and he was having a hard time controlling his emotions.

He had lost several friends when a Lancaster bomber flying on a mission over France had crashed and burned. The thing was the aircraft had not been hit by enemy fire. A manufacturing defect had caused it "to fall out of the sky." He explained it but I was too young to understand. But I understood his objective. He was speaking for his dead comrades, urging the workers to be more diligent, to recognize that the Lancaster bomber could well be the key to England's victory or defeat.

He was magnificent. I was deeply moved, as were the men who stood there listening. From that day on I held airmen in the highest regard. When I had to serve my national service years later I selected the RAF.

On active service: *A British R.A.F. airman,*
wearing his battle dress.

The Nightmare

The third war-related happening had all the elements of a nightmare – quite literally, because it occurred in the middle of the night.

The Germans, it seemed, shared the same view as the airman on the wooden box when it came to assessing the Lancaster bomber. They decided to bomb the Austin Motor Company into oblivion.

It was not an easy objective. The Austin Motor Company was located in the "midlands", the heart and center of England. To get there they had to avoid fighter aircraft and, on the ground, anti-aircraft gun batteries. The improbability of their getting through to the Austin Motor Company was sufficiently strong that the factory had little or no air defence. The one exception was the large barrage balloons, filled with helium gas, that lurked unseen in the dark at strategic points around the factory.

I don't know how many planes made it through but there had to be several. As previously mentioned, the Austin Motor Company was down the road from where Aunt Nell lived.

The nightmare must have begun before I actually awoke because the first thing I remember is coming out of a deep sleep and being aware of loud noise and a woman screaming.

As I opened my eyes there was the biggest bang I had ever heard in my life and the room was filled with an intense white light.

I could see Aunt Nell sitting on Michael's bed. Michael was sitting up and Aunt Nell had him clasped to her breast. She was screaming, "Don't be scared! Don't be scared!"

There was another loud bang and the entire night sky outside the bedroom window lit up.

"They're crashing into the barrage balloons," screamed Aunt Nell.

Gas filled barrage balloons that were raised to different heights to foil enemy aircraft.

I had the feeling that I was some sort of distant spectator. Aunt Nell and Michael seemed to be wholly unaware that I was even in the room. It was uncanny. I realized that I was on my own again and in a strange sort of way I was quite calm.

I wanted to get out of bed and look out the window to see what was going on. I thought about it but a loud explosion, followed by another, persuaded me that it wasn't a good idea. Then the window rattled and the house shook.

It was at this moment that I remembered Exmouth.

Now I was terrified. I could see in my mind's eye the devastation left by the air-raid in Exmouth. Was I going to be blown to smithereens? Would it hurt?

I was suddenly aware that I was powerless to do anything so I did the only intelligent thing I could think of: I hid under the bed covers and rolled myself into a tight ball – a very small and very tight ball.

The next day I went down to the factory to see what had happened.

It was astonishing. The factory was still there! Black smoke was curling into the air from an area of the plant behind the main gate that I couldn't see. If I remember correctly there were two or three gaping holes in the building, with twisted metal and broken glass in the area of the holes, but the overall factory (which was a big building) seemed in good shape. I saw no evidence of aircraft wreckage or remnants of barrage balloons.

It was puzzling. I shook my head and slowly walked back to Aunt Nell's.

Off To London

My life with Aunt Nell came to an end in dramatic fashion.

Towards the end of the war my father suddenly appeared. He said he planned to re-marry and introduced his "intended" to Aunt Nell. The two women took an immediate and intense dislike to one another. Aunt Nell then conveyed to my father that he should not, under any circumstance, marry "that woman".

I guess my father wasn't listening because some time after that Aunt Nell flew into a rage. She packed a suitcase and told me that we were going to London. My next memory is the sight of Aunt Nell pushing the door bell of a house in London. A woman with a baby in her arms came to the door.

Aunt Nell said simply: "Here. He's yours." She then turned on her heel and walked away.

Aunt Nell's departure marked the beginning

of another unhappy period. I have decided, however, to let that period slip away from my memory. Well almost…

My New Mother

There's one recollection that speaks to the nature of the period.

*A **female air-raid warden** gives comfort to a child rescued from a bombed building.*

There was an air-raid one night and the next morning we were all sitting around the breakfast table. The adults were excited because bombs had destroyed a number of houses a few streets away and they knew some of the people who had been "bombed out."

They then looked at me and began to laugh.

"Bombed out" residents take stock of their homes after an air raid.

I was unaware that there had been an air raid and had no idea why they were laughing.

They then explained:

It seems that I was sound asleep when the air-raid siren began to wail. My "new mother' had tried to wake me but I had apparently rolled over in my sleep and said: "I'm alright. I've got my money-box (piggy-bank) under the pillow." They left me there and made their way to the air raid shelter outside the house that was at the end of the garden.

Years later I wondered how my new mother

A woman trapped in her bombed home is pulled to safety. She lived.

would have explained it to my father if the house, with me in it, had been destroyed.

I also found out, years later, that after the war my new mother urged my father to place me in a home for unwanted boys. It was called Dr. Barnardo's Home.

My father refused.

Anyway, I want to move on and briefly mention the beginning of my teenage years. The period was war related because it represented the aftermath of my wartime childhood.

Children sent to an orphanage, *following their parents being killed.*

Mr. Hughes

At the end of the war we lived in Wimbledon. I went to a "nothing school" in a poor area which was somewhat appropriate because I was a nothing person myself. I was awkward, clumsy, had no self-confidence, and was wholly deficient when it came to applying personal relationship skills. The school, on the other hand, had one thing going for it. The headmaster was a "leading educational figure." His name was Fielden Hughes. He wrote about education for several newspapers, had written an adventure book for boys, and was on the BBC radio from time to time.

For some reason or another he took a liking to me.

The school was chosen to be an experimental school for something called "comprehensive secondary education." The year was 1947. I was 13 years old.

One day the older boys at the school, myself included, were told to make their way to the main assembly hall. We were told that large white circles had been drawn on the floor denoting various "educational pursuits." We were told that we should select one of the circles and sit down inside it. One of the circles was for GARDENING and I went and sat down with several other boys.

I then noticed a large circle identified as JOURNALISM. A boy sitting near me said that Mr. Hughes would be teaching the course. I didn't know what journalism was all about but I liked Mr. Hughes.

I got up, crossed the floor, and sat down in the journalism circle.

It was a quick mental decision, followed by an immediate and impetuous act. It involved, at most, ten seconds. I look back now and marvel at the luck and enormity of it.

I took to journalism as a duck takes to water. My ability and confidence grew in tandem. I went from being the class dunce to a top student -- and not only in journalism. I began to excel in other subjects as well. It was amazing. The key of course lay in the fact that someone believed in me (Mr. Hughes) and I eventually discovered that I had reason to believe in myself.

A feature of the experimental school was that you had the option of staying in school for an extra year. When the time came my stepmother was vehemently opposed to the idea. She said that I ought to be "earning my keep" and should get a job at the local toy factory.

My father won out for a second time. He argued that if Mr. Hughes thought I had the necessary ability and could "make it", I should be given the opportunity.

And make it I did – first as a junior reporter on a weekly south London newspaper, then as a reporter on a daily newspaper in Canada. I emigrated to Canada in 1956. I next became a trade journal editor.

In 1964 I went into business for myself. I launched a small trade journal publishing company. It still exists although I no longer own it. It still carries my name however.

I retired from business in 1990.

Pamela

I can't conclude this memoir without mentioning one other person. Her name was Pamela.

In her own way she changed my life as much (and perhaps even more) than Mr. Hughes. It was more than first love. We were soulmates. With Pamela I emerged from the inner darkness of myself. I smiled, joked, developed a personality. I think it can be said that I even became a "fun person."

I remember, exactly, how the change began.

It wasn't the day we met. It was some time later. I bought her a bouquet of flowers. It wasn't a big bouquet, just a small bunch of spring flowers. I took them to her house and knocked on the door.

Her face said it all.

There was astonishment but also a look of immense delight and pleasure. At the same time she seemed overwhelmed. She stumbled, trying to find adequate words to express her appreciation. I was taken aback. How could she be that happy? It was just a bunch of spring flowers. Her eyes were moist and Oh, dear God, she was so incredibly beautiful.

I don't recall what happened next. But I do recall how I felt when I left her house. I was delirious! I had made an incredible discovery. *I now knew how to relate to people!*

It was easy. All it took was kindness and consideration. All you had to do was think of someone else as opposed to yourself.

It was astonishing the way it worked.

You made someone happy and you felt good inside. And there was something else. A bond was created. They did nice things for you. It was a two-way street.

The sad part, of course, was that I had to be sixteen years of age to make the discovery.

Epilogue

It has been suggested, in post-war literature, that most evacuees enjoyed the experience of being evacuated; that they were delighted to leave behind the deplorable living conditions of their inner-city homes; that "life in the country" was an exciting and mind broadening experience. It has been further suggested that "only a minority" were mistreated – the inference being that it was, overall, a small and insignificant problem.

This mythical perception of the evacuation is unfortunate.

Successful societies learn from their history. They recognize and assess their mistakes; they view mistakes as learning opportunities. The end product of this activity is new and innovative thinking that leads, more often than not, to new programs and concepts to better serve society.

History denied (or misrepresented) is opporunity lost.

This epilogue has two objectives: The first is to offer a more accurate perspective in respect to the evacuation. The second is to draw attention to an important and useful lesson that can be extracted from the evacuation.

No one knows, for sure, the number of U.K. children evacuated during the war. The most frequently quoted figure is 3,000,000. Some have suggested that the figure was closer to 3,500,000. Others have made the point that a large number of evacuees returned to the cities when bombing didn't immediately occur at the outbreak of war and were re-evacuated when bombing did commence. A minimum conservative figure of 1,500,000 is perhaps the closest figure to reality that can be established.

Knowing the 1.5 million figure is important for this reason:

BBC History has an interesting article in its archives that mentions research findings of author David Prest, a BBC journalist/producer. The article was written in 1999. Prest spoke to almost 450 ex-evacuees for a radio program that he was producing. The following is taken from the article:

"The present writer spoke
directly to nearly 450 ex-
evacuees, and of these 12
percent say they suffered
some sort of mental,
physical or specifically
sexual abuse, as defined by
the children's welfare
organizations of today.

"Naturally, and sadly,
deep scars lie just below
the surface of that
minority."

Twelve percent seems an insignificant
figure – until you apply it to 1.5 million children.
Simple math tells us that 12 percent equals 180,000
children.

We can attempt to ease our discomfort at
the enormity of this figure by questioning the un-
scientific method used to produce it. But here's
another statistic: Scholars and researchers are of the
opinion that the number of evacuees mistreated was
15%. That translates into 225,000 children.

The suffering of those who were abused is not

something that should be passed over lightly. But there is something further that needs to be said: *The abuse was part of a much bigger picture* – a perpetrated "wrong" that impacted not only those who were abused but many thousands more.

This is what happened:

> *Many evacuees were taken in because those accepting the children felt they had a civic and patriotic duty to do so. They gave shelter – but many saw this as the extent of their patriotic duty.*
>
> *They did not feel an obligation to act as surrogate parents. As a consequence, many evacuees grew up in an emotional vacuum without the benefit of social nurturing.*
>
> *There was no one to offer advice, motivation, or encouragement. There*

was no one to explain social
values. There was no one
to give them a sense of
self-worth.

An overlooked tragedy
of the great evacuation was
that thousands of young
people grew up to be some-
thing less than what they
might have been, due to an
absence of parental guid-
ance and encouragement.

How should we react to this knowledge?
What should we feel? What, if anything, should we
do?

The immediate and instinctive response is
to feel sorry for those caught up in the tragedy.
The next response, again instinctive, is to wonder
whether we can put things right in some manner.
We realize however that too much time has passed.
It seems, superficially at least, that we can't do
anything except to feel sorry. But this is an incorrect
assumption.

We can *learn* from what happened. There
is a "truth" that becomes all the more focused and

meaningful *if we consider it with the wartime evacu-ation in mind.* This is the truth:

> *The strength of a*
> *society is the people that*
> *comprise it.*
>
> *To the extent that*
> *each individual is allowed*
> *to reach his or her full*
> *potential, the society is*
> *enriched.*
>
> *Conversely however,*
> *when one or more*
> *individuals are prevented*
> *from being all that they*
> *might have been, the*
> *society experiences a*
> *loss.*
>
> *It is in a society's*
> *best interest to seek,*
> *assist, and generally*
> *encourage the full*
> *development of its*
> *young.*

But how?

There is a limit to what a government can legislate. There is a limit to what it can demand. There is a limit to the programs that it can implement.

Parenting is the key.

You can't however legislate parenting that is loving, wise, and socially responsible.

What then is the answer?

The solution recommended by this epilogue is to teach and influence those who will be *tomorrow's* parents, the young people of *today*.

But what, specifically, should we teach them? The answer, in the author's view, is *social nurturing* that we can define as follows:

> *Social nurturing is*
> ***mentoring.*** *It is the act*
> *of conveying to a young*
> *person that you believe*
> *in them; that you consider*
> *them to be of value; that*
> *you care about their*
> *welfare; that you are willing*
> *to stand by them, aid their*
> *development, and share*

your expertise and
knowledge with them.

Social nurturing is
exhortation. *It is the act*
of encouraging and
urging a young person
to be the best that he or
she can be.

Social nurturing is
engendering belief. *It is*
the act of lauding the
institutions that define a
democratic society;
it is the act of creating
faith, trust, and pride, in
democratic institutions.

It is for others to decide how social nurturing can best be taught. The following however is offered for consideration:

ONE BOY'S STORY
has the power to inform
and motivate in a
simplistic manner.

It can be read and absorbed in less than 40 minutes.

It could be used in a classroom setting to generate debate and discussion.

ISBN 142512052-0